pg. 1-8
(2-12)

Practice & Assess

Test Preparation

Geometry

PRENTICE HALL MATHEMATICS

GEOMETRY

PEARSON

Prentice Hall

Needham, Massachusetts
Upper Saddle River, New Jersey

What Does This Book Do?

This book has been designed specifically to help you prepare for mathematics assessment by reviewing this year's mathematics content with special emphasis on reasoning skills that are so important in high-stakes testing. You will gain confidence in your test-taking skills as you work through the various sections in this book.

Chapter Practice

This section contains chapter-by-chapter practice in standardized test format to help you identify what you have learned as well as which topics you need to review and study further. With chapter-specific content, these tests are designed to give you continued test practice throughout the school year.

End-of-Course Test Practice

This section of the book enables you to practice test taking with a mixed review of only the mathematics in this year's curriculum. This test's multiple-choice format will help you prepare for end-of-course tests as well as other high-stakes tests.

SAT/ACT Mathematics Practice

This section of the book provides you with the highlights of both the SAT and ACT as they relate to mathematics. It also includes invaluable test-taking strategies to help you gain confidence in your test-taking skills. Finally, there is a Practice Test with questions in several formats - multiple-choice, quantitative comparison, and student-produced response - so you can assess your knowledge and test-taking skills.

Together, these sections will give you solid practice with the types of questions and the mathematical content that you are likely to see on numerous high-stakes tests.

Cover Photo: Digital Imagery 2001 © PhotoDisc, Inc.

PEARSON
Prentice
Hall

ISBN 0-13-068641-7
2 3 4 5 6 7 8 9 10   06 05 04 03

Table of Contents

● **Chapter Practice**

SAT/ACT Preparation

Chapter Practice

Chapter 1

For Exercises 1–15, choose the correct letter.

1. Which of the following is next in the sequence?
$1, 5, 9, 13, 17, \underline{\ ?\ }$

A 20   **B** 21   **C** 22   **D** 23

E none of the above

2. Which is the next figure in the sequence?

, , ,

A   **B**   **C**

D   **E** none of the above

3. Which of the following points is not collinear with the other points?

A $(1, 0)$ **B** $(2, 2)$ **C** $(3, 3)$ **D** $(0, -2)$

E none of the above

4. Which segment is not parallel to $\overline{AD}$?

A $\overline{BC}$ **B** $\overline{FG}$ **C** $\overline{EH}$ **D** $\overline{EF}$

E none of the above

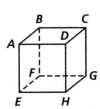

5. If $TV = 45$, find the value of x.

A 2   **B** 3   **C** 4   **D** 5

E none of the above

6. The coordinates of the midpoint of $\overline{LN}$ with endpoints $L(-1, -3)$ and $N(3, -5)$ are

A $(1, -4)$ **B** $(-2, 1)$

C $(-1, -4)$ **D** $(1, 4)$

E none of the above

7. $\overrightarrow{OF}$ bisects $\angle EOG$. Which of the following is *not* true?

A $m\angle EOF = m\angle FOG$

B $m\angle FOG = \frac{1}{2}m\angle EOG$

C $m\angle FOG = m\angle EOG - m\angle EOF$

D $\angle EOF \cong \angle EOG$

E none of the above

8. What is the radius of a circle with diameter $2\sqrt{2}$?

A $\dfrac{\sqrt{2}}{2}$ **B** $\sqrt{2}$

C $4\sqrt{2}$ **D** $\dfrac{\sqrt{2}}{4}$

E none of the above

9. The perimeter of a rectangle is 30 in. and the base is 10 in. What is the area?

A 15 in.^{2}

B 40 in.^{2}

C 150 in.^{2}

D 300 in.^{2}

E none of the above

10. Find the area of the shaded portion of the figure. All angles in the figure are right angles.

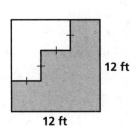

A 48 ft^2

B 96 ft^2

C 108 ft^2

D 144 ft^2

E not enough information

11. Estimate the measure of ∠QRS.

A 115°   B 95°

C 75°   D 55°

E none of the above

12. The intersection of planes
FBE and ACD is

A $\overleftrightarrow{BC}$ B $\overline{BC}$

C point B

D point B and point C

E none of the above

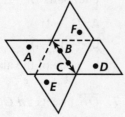

13. A business card is approximately 9 cm by 5 cm. How many square centimeters of paper are used to create a deck of 45 cards?

A 45 cm²

B 90 cm²

C 2025 cm²

D 2250 cm²

E none of the above

14. The perimeter of parallelogram HIJK is 32 in. If HI = 12 in., find the length of HK.

A 4 in.

B 8 in.

C 12 in.

D 20 in.

E none of the above

15. What is the distance between (−5, −3) and (4, −7)?

A 9.8

B 10.0

C 2.2

D 18.9

E none of the above

For Exercises 16–19, compare the boxed quantity in Column A with the boxed quantity in Column B. Choose the best answer.

A The quantity in Column A is greater.

B The quantity in Column B is greater.

C The two quantities are equal.

D The relationship cannot be determined on the basis of the information supplied.

<u>Column A</u>	<u>Column B</u>

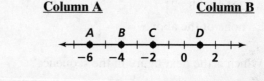

16.

AC	BD

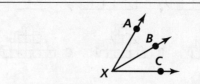

17.

m∠AXB	m∠BXC

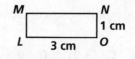

18.

perimeter of rectangle LMNO	perimeter of square HIJK

19.

area of rectangle LMNO	area of square HIJK

For Exercises 20–22, write your answer.

20. Find the distance between A(6, 2) and B(−2, 8).

21. Find the radius and the coordinates of the center for each circle with diameter $\overline{AB}$.

a. A(2, 0), B(2, 4)   **b.** A(−1, 2), B(−1, 4)

22. **Open-ended** Draw an obtuse angle. Construct its angle bisector.

Name _____ Class _____ Date _____

Chapter Practice

Chapter 2

For Exercises 1–7, choose the correct letter.

1. $m\angle AXB = 49$,
$m\angle BXC = 3y + 3$, and
$m\angle AXC = 11y + 4$.
Find the value of y.

  A 6

  B 3

  C −6.25

  D 7

  E none of the above

2. $m\angle WOX = 2x + 1$
and $m\angle XOY = 3x - 9$.
Find $m\angle WOY$.

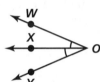

  A 10

  B 21

  C 42

  D 52

  E none of the above

3. Two acute angles can be which of the following?

    I. vertical
    II. adjacent
    III. complementary
    IV. supplementary

  A I and II   **B** I, II, and III
  C I and III   **D** I, II, and IV
  E none of the above

4. Evaluate $2(b^2 - 4b) + 3$ for $b = 4$.

  A 0   **B** 2   **C** 3   **D** −16
  E none of the above

5. What is the converse of this statement?
If a polygon is a hexagon, then the polygon has six sides.

  A If a polygon is not a hexagon, then the polygon does not have six sides.

  B If a polygon does not have six sides, then the polygon is not a hexagon.

  C If a polygon has six sides, then the polygon is a hexagon.

  D A polygon is a hexagon if and only if it has six sides.

  E none of the above

6. The total cost for bus tickets for a family equals the number of adults at $1.00 each plus the number of children at $.50 each. Which equation could be used to model this?

  A $T = c(a + 0.5)$

  B $c = 1a + 0.5c$

  C $T = 1a + 0.5c$

  D $c = a(1 + 0.5c)$

  E $T = 1.5a + c$

7. If a square's side is 5 cm, then its area is 25 cm². Which of the following statements are true?

    I. "If a square's side is 5 cm" is the hypothesis.
    II. "If a square's side is 5 cm" is the conclusion.
    III. "Then its area is 25 cm²" is the hypothesis.
    IV. "Then its area is 25 cm²" is the conclusion.

  A I only

  B II only

  C I and IV only

  D II and III only

  E I, II, and III

For Exercises 8–10, compare the boxed quantity in Column A with the boxed quantity in Column B. Choose the best answer.

A The quantity in Column A is greater.

B The quantity in Column B is greater.

C The two quantities are equal.

D The relationship cannot be determined on the basis of the information supplied.

<u>Column A</u>   <u>Column B</u>

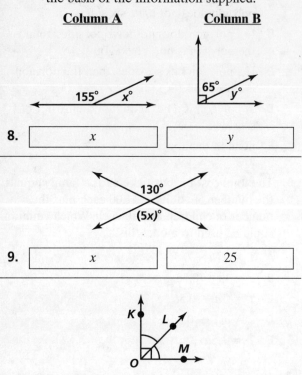

| 8. | x | y |

| 9. | x | 25 |

| 10. | $m\angle KOL$ | measure of the complement of $m\angle LOM$ |

For Exercises 11–15, write your answer.

11. One angle is twice as large as its supplement. Find the measure of the larger angle.

12. What can you conclude from the diagram? Justify your answer.

13. **Open-ended** Draw a line. Then draw a second line that intersects the first. Describe the relationships among the angles formed by the two lines.

14. Write the converse of the statement: "If two angles are supplementary, then the sum of their measures is 180°."

15. Write the two conditionals contained in the statement: "A runner wins a race if and only if she runs the fastest."

Chapter Practice

Chapter 3

For Exercises 1–11, choose the correct letter.

1. What is $m\angle EFG$?

   A 69   **B** 79

   C 100   **D** 101

   E none of the above

   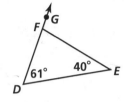

2. If $m\angle L = 45$ and $m\angle M = 45$, $\triangle LMN$ is classified as what kind of triangle?

   A acute scalene   **B** obtuse isosceles

   C acute isosceles   **D** right isosceles

   E none of the above

3. The measures of the angles of a quadrilateral are shown below. In which case is x not an integer?

   A $x, x, 2x, 3x$ **B** $2x, 2x, 3x, 3x$

   C $2x, 3x, 4x, 6x$ **D** $x, 2x, 3x, 3x$

   E none of the above

4. Find the measure of one of the interior angles of the regular polygon shown.

   A 60   **B** 120

   C 135   **D** 145

   E none of the above

5. Which of these lines is perpendicular to the line $y = 2x + 6$?

   A $2y = -4x + 3$ **B** $2y = 4x + 3$

   C $2y = x + 3$ **D** $-2y = x + 3$

   E none of the above

6. A triangle has angle measures of $2x + 10$, $4x$, and $5x + 5$. What are the measures of each angle from smallest to largest?

   A 40, 60, 80   **B** 45, 50, 85

   C 30, 40, 110   **D** 20, 70, 90

   E none of the above

7. If the length of the sides of a triangle are 12, 12, and 16, how would the triangle be classified?

   A acute isosceles   **B** obtuse isosceles

   C isosceles right   **D** acute scalene

   E none of the above

8. How should $\angle 1$ and $\angle 2$ be classified?

   A alternate interior angles

   B corresponding angles

   C same-side interior angles

   D vertical angles

   E none of the above

9. If parallel lines are cut by a transversal, what could be the measures of two of their same-side interior angles?

      I. 30 and 150   II. 60 and 60

   III. 105 and 105   IV. 42 and 138

   A I only   **B** II only

   C III only   **D** I and II

   E none of the above

10. If you select one even-numbered angle and one odd-numbered angle from the diagram, what is the probability that the two angles are congruent? Assume that the transversal is not perpendicular to the parallel lines.

    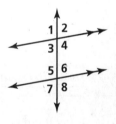

    A $\frac{1}{8}$ **B** $\frac{1}{4}$ **C** $\frac{1}{2}$ **D** $\frac{3}{4}$

    E none of the above

11. Which of the following statements is true?

   A The slope of a vertical line is zero.

   B A line through the origin and (2, −1) has a negative slope.

   C All lines through the origin have an undefined slope.

   D A line through (1, 1) and (−1, 3) has a positive slope.

   E none of the above

For Exercises 12–16, compare the boxed quantity in Column A with the boxed quantity in Column B. Choose the best answer.

   A The quantity in Column A is greater.

   B The quantity in Column B is greater.

   C The two quantities are equal.

   D The relationship cannot be determined on the basis of the information supplied.

<u>Column A</u>   <u>Column B</u>

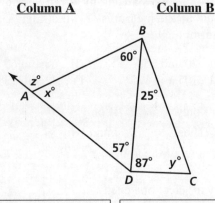

12. | x | y |

13. | $m\angle ABD + m\angle BDA$ | z |

14. | the number of pairs of same-side interior angles formed by two parallel lines and a transversal | the number of pairs of alternate interior angles formed by two parallel line and a transversal |

<u>Column A</u>   <u>Column B</u>

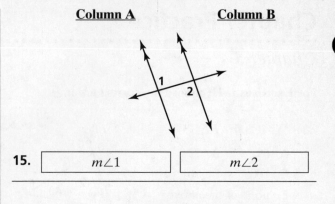

15. | $m\angle 1$ | $m\angle 2$ |

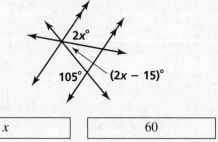

16. | x | 60 |

For Exercises 17–20, write your answer.

17. **Writing** Explain how you can determine if two lines are parallel, perpendicular, or neither.

18. **Writing** Given only the measures of a triangle's sides, explain how to determine whether the triangle is acute, obtuse, or right.

19. Find $m\angle 1$ and then $m\angle 2$. State the theorems or postulates that justify your answer.

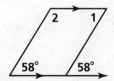

20. **Writing** Describe three pairs of angles that can be used to determine whether two lines are parallel. Include a diagram.

Name_____ Class_____ Date_____

Chapter Practice

Chapter 4

For Exercises 1–8, choose the correct letter.

1. $\triangle STU \cong \triangle HIJ$. Which of the following can be the coordinates of point U?

   A (6, −3)
   B (5, −2)
   C (6, −4)
   D (0, −4)
   E none of the above

   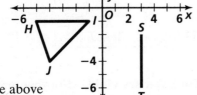

2. What can you conclude from this diagram?

   A Both triangles are equiangular.
   B $\angle A \cong \angle CBD$
   C $\angle A \cong \angle C$
   D $\overline{CD} \cong \overline{BD}$
   E none of the above

   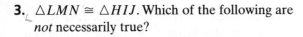

3. $\triangle LMN \cong \triangle HIJ$. Which of the following are *not* necessarily true?

   I. $\angle L \cong \angle H$ II. $\overline{LM} \cong \overline{IJ}$
   III. $\angle N \cong \angle I$ IV. $\overline{LN} \cong \overline{HJ}$

   A I and II   B II and III
   C III and IV   D I and IV
   E none of the above

4. By which theorem or postulate are the triangles congruent?

   A AAS   B SAS   C AAA   D HL
   E none of the above

5. Which statements can you use to prove $\triangle PEG \cong \triangle HAT$ by the ASA Postulate?

   I. $\overline{PE} \cong \overline{HA}$
   II. $\angle P \cong \angle H$
   III. $\overline{PG} \cong \overline{HT}$
   IV. $\angle G \cong \angle T$

   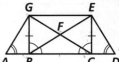

   A I, II, and IV   B I, III, and IV
   C II, III, and I   D I, II, and IV
   E none of the above

6. Which two triangles in the diagram are congruent by SAS?

   A $\triangle GAB \cong \triangle EDC$
   B $\triangle BFC \cong \triangle GFE$
   C $\triangle BGF \cong \triangle CEF$
   D $\triangle BGC \cong \triangle CEB$
   E none of the above

7. What additional information would you need to prove $\triangle NOT \cong \triangle NET$ by the HL Theorem?

   A $\overline{NO} \cong \overline{NE}$
   B $\angle OTN \cong \angle ETN$
   C $NT = 2NO$
   D $\overline{NO} \cong \overline{TE}$
   E none of the above

   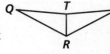

8. Which pair of conditions does *not* provide enough information to prove that $\triangle QRT \cong \triangle SRT$?

   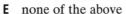

   I. $\angle Q \cong \angle S$ II. $\angle QTR \cong \angle STR$
   III. $\overline{QT} \cong \overline{ST}$ IV. $\overline{QR} \cong \overline{SR}$

   A I and II   B II and III
   C III and IV   D I and IV
   E none of the above

For Exercises 9–14, compare the boxed quantity in Column A with the boxed quantity in Column B. Choose the best answer.

A The quantity in Column A is greater.

B The quantity in Column B is greater.

C The two quantities are equal.

D The relationship cannot be determined on the basis of the information supplied.

<u>Column A</u>   <u>Column B</u>

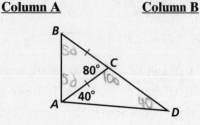

9. | $m\angle CBA$ | | $m\angle CAD$ |

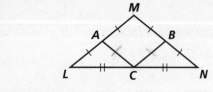

10. | AC | | BC |

11. | LM | | $2 \cdot BC$ |

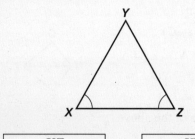

12. | XZ | | XY |

<u>Column A</u>   <u>Column B</u>

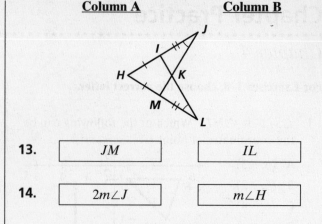

13. | JM | | IL |

14. | $2m\angle J$ | | $m\angle H$ |

For Exercises 15–18, write your answer.

15. Which theorem or postulate would be easiest to use to prove $\triangle ABC \cong \triangle EDC$?

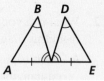

16. Write a two column proof.

Given: O is the midpoint of $\overline{AC}$ and of $\overline{BD}$.

Prove: $\triangle AOD \cong \triangle COB$

17. **Open-ended** Two flower beds are shaped like right triangles. What measurements could you make to show that the two triangular flower beds are congruent? Explain.

18. The tree at the right is perpendicular to the ground containing points B, C, D, and E. The support wires running from the tree to points B, C, and D are the same length. Is this enough information to conclude that $\triangle AEB$, $\triangle AEC$, and $\triangle AED$ are congruent? Explain.

Chapter Practice

Chapter 5

For Exercises 1–8, choose the correct letter.

1. A quadrilateral's diagonal is 16 cm long. What is the length of a midsegment parallel to this diagonal?

   A 8 cm   **B** 32 cm   **C** 16 cm   **D** 4 cm

   E none of the above

2. What is the inverse of this statement?
   If it is warm outside, then we drink water.

   A If we drink water, then it is warm outside.

   B If we do not drink water, then it is not warm outside.

   C We drink water if and only if it is warm outside.

   D If it is not warm outside, then we do not drink water.

   E none of the above

3. Which could *not* be the lengths of the sides of a triangle?

   A 1, 4, 4   **B** 1, 11, 12   **C** 3, 5, 7

   D 8, 11, 18   **E** none of the above

4. For what type of triangle is the point of concurrency of the altitudes outside the triangle?

   A right triangle   **B** obtuse triangle

   C acute triangle   **D** equilateral triangle

   E none of the above

5. What can you *not* conclude based on the figure below?

   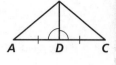

   A $\triangle ABD \cong \triangle CBD$

   B $\overline{BD}$ is the perpendicular bisector of $\overline{AC}$.

   C $\triangle ABC$ is isosceles.

   D $\overline{AB} \cong \overline{BC}$

   E none of the above

6. Find the value of *x*.

   A 12   **B** 16.3

   C 15   **D** 18

   E none of the above

7. Which of the following is true?

   A $\frac{1}{2} < -\frac{1}{3}$ **B** $\frac{1}{4} < \frac{1}{3}$

   C $-\frac{1}{2} > -\frac{1}{4}$ **D** $-\frac{1}{4} > \frac{1}{3}$

   E none of the above

8. Which of the following inequalities can be represented by this number line?

   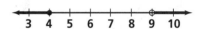

   A $4 < b < 9$ **B** $9 \leq b \leq 4$

   C $b \leq 9$ or $b > 4$ **D** $b \leq 4$ or $b > 9$

   E $b < 4$ and $b > 9$

For Exercises 9–11, compare the boxed quantity in Column A with the boxed quantity in Column B. Choose the best answer.

A   The quantity in Column A is greater.

B   The quantity in Column B is greater.

C   The two quantities are equal.

D   The relationship cannot be determined on the basis of the information supplied.

Column A	Column B

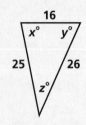

9. | x | y |

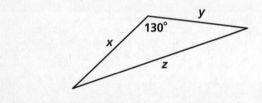

10. | $x^2 + y^2$ | z^2 |

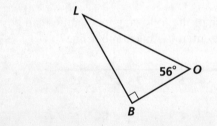

11. | LB | OB |

For Exercises 12–15, write your answer.

12.   **Open-ended** Draw a triangle, and draw its angle bisectors. Then construct the circle inscribed in the triangle.

13.   Leroy is delivering flowers to houses C and D on Bemis Road, as shown below. At what location (E) should he park his car so that $CE + DE$ is as small as possible? Show how you found E.

————————————————————— **Bemis Road**

14.   Use indirect reasoning to prove the statement:
      If Marcus sells three sandwiches for more than $12, then at least one of the sandwiches costs more than $4.

15.   Perimeter of ABC = 32 cm. Find n.

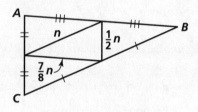

Chapter Practice

Chapter 6

For Exercises 1–10, choose the correct letter.

1. What is the most precise name for a quadrilateral with vertices $(2, -1), (6, 3), (-2, 3),$ and $(2, 9)$?

   A rectangle   B parallelogram

   C kite   D rhombus

   E none of the above

2. What is a name for the quadrilateral below?

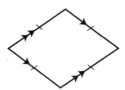

   I. rectangle   II. square
   III. rhombus   IV. parallelogram

   A I and II   B I, III, and IV

   C III and IV   D IV only

   E none of the above

3. Determine the value of x for which *TARP* is a parallelogram.

   A 3
   B 4
   C 5
   D 6
   E none of the above

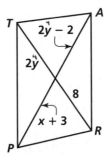

4. Which is sufficient to prove that a quadrilateral is a rhombus?

   A The diagonals bisect each other.

   B The diagonals are perpendicular.

   C All four sides are congruent.

   D A pair of opposite sides are congruent and parallel.

   E none of the above

5. If two angles of an isosceles trapezoid are randomly selected, what is the probability that they will be supplementary?

   A $\frac{3}{4}$ B $\frac{2}{3}$ C $\frac{1}{2}$ D $\frac{1}{4}$

   E none of the above

6. Find the value of m in parallelogram *WXYZ*.

   A 40   B 45
   C 90   D 135

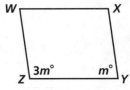

7. Which figure does *not* have diagonals that bisect each other?

   A parallelogram   B isosceles trapezoid

   C square   D rhombus

   E all of the above

8. In quadrilateral *BCDE*, $\angle B$ is congruent to $\angle E$. How could *BCDE not* be classified?

   A square   B trapezoid

   C kite   D rectangle

   E none of the above

9. Give the coordinates for point *R* without using any new variables.

   A $(-c - a, b)$
   B $(-c + a, b)$
   C $(c - a, b)$
   D $(-c - a, -b)$
   E none of the above

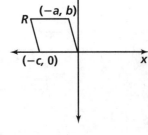

10. What is the measure of the midsegment of trapezoid *STUV*?

    A 6.5 cm
    B 7 cm
    C 8 cm
    D 9 cm
    E none of the above

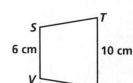

For Exercises 11–15, compare the boxed quantity in Column A with the boxed quantity in Column B. Choose the best answer.

A The quantity in Column A is greater.

B The quantity in Column B is greater.

C The two quantities are equal.

D The relationship cannot be determined on the basis of the information supplied.

Column A	Column B

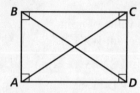

11.

AC	BD

12.

percent of change when \$750 is discounted to \$690	percent of change when \$75 is discounted to \$69

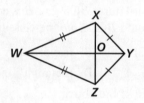

13.

$m\angle XOY$	89

14.

WZ	$2 \cdot ZY$

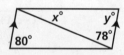

15.

x	y

For Exercises 16–21, write your answer.

16. Open-ended Given $ABCD$ is a square, use a paragraph proof, flow proof, two-column proof, or coordinate geometry to show that $\overline{AC} \cong \overline{BD}$.

17. Writing Explain how to find the measures of the remaining three angles of an isosceles trapezoid if you already know the measure of one of the angles.

18. Points $D(1, 1)$, $E(2, 3)$, $F(6, 3)$, and $G(5, 1)$ are the coordinates of a quadrilateral.

   a. Sketch the quadrilateral in a coordinate plane.

   b. Find the quadrilateral's perimeter.

   c. Find the quadrilateral's area.

19. Find the values of the variables.

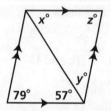

20. Open-ended Sketch two non-congruent parallelograms $XYZW$ and $STUV$ such that $\overline{XZ} \cong \overline{YW} \cong \overline{SU} \cong \overline{TV}$.

21. $ABCD$ is a parallelogram. Give the coordinates of C without using any new variables.

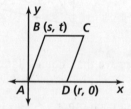

Chapter Practice

Chapter 7

For Exercises 1–9, choose the correct letter.

1. Which of the following is equivalent to
$3n - 4 = -5n + 9$?

A $8n - 9 = -4$

B $4 + 3n = 5n - 9$

C $-5n - 9 = 3n + 4$

D $8n - 4 = 9$

E none of the above

2. Find the area of rhombus *LMNO*.

A 16 cm^2

B $8\sqrt{3}$ cm^2

C 8 cm^2

D $4\sqrt{3}$ cm^2

E none of the above

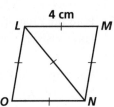

3. A circle has radius 12 cm. The central angle of a sector measures 150. What is the area of the sector?

A 60π cm^2

B 10π cm^2

C 144π cm^2

D 67.5π cm^2

E none of the above

4. Find the area of the triangle enclosed by the lines $x = 0$, $y = 5$, and $y = -x$.

A 12 square units

B $12\frac{1}{2}$ square units

C 25 square units

D 37 square units

E none of the above

5. Find the area of the shaded region.

A $4\pi + 16$ cm^2

B $4\pi - 16$ cm^2

C $16 - 4\pi$ cm^2

D $16\pi - 16$ cm^2

E none of the above

6. Which of the following can be the length of the sides of a 45°-45°-90° triangle?

I. $\frac{1}{2}, 1, \frac{\sqrt{3}}{2}$

II. $2, 2, 2\sqrt{2}$

III. $3, 3, 3\sqrt{3}$

A I only   B II only   C III only

D II and III

E none of the above

7. One base of a trapezoid is three times as long as the other. The height is the average of the two bases. If the area of the trapezoid is 64 yd^2, find the length of the longer base.

A 4 yd   B 8 yd   C 12 yd   D 16 yd

E none of the above

8. Jamal and Grace are going to divide a slice of pizza evenly. The measure of the pizza slice's arc is 60 and the radius of the pizza is 9 in. Find the arc length of Grace's slice.

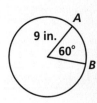

A 1.5π in.   B 3π in.

C 6π in.   D 9π in.

E none of the above

9. Find the area of the shaded region.

A $(32 - 16\pi)$ cm

B $(16\pi - 32)$ cm

C $(64 - 32\pi)$ cm

D $(32\pi - 64)$ cm

E none of the above

For Exercises 10–12, compare the boxed quantity in Column A with the boxed quantity in Column B. Choose the best answer.

A The quantity in Column A is greater.

B The quantity in Column B is greater.

C The two quantities are equal.

D The relationship cannot be determined on the basis of the information supplied.

<u>Column A</u>   <u>Column B</u>

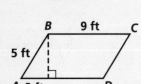

10. | area of parallelogram *ABCD* | area of trapezoid *WXYZ* |

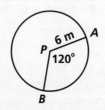

11. | diameter of ⊙*P* | (Use π = 3.14) length of $\widehat{AB}$ |

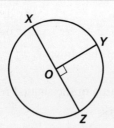

12. | $m\widehat{XY}$ | $m\widehat{YZ}$ |

For Exercises 13–16, write your answer.

13. Open-ended Sketch a trapezoid whose area is 30 m². Label the measures of its height and bases.

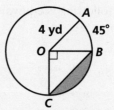

For Exercises 14 and 15.

14. Find the area of sector *AOB*. Leave your answer in terms of π.

15. Find the area of the shaded segment. Leave your answer in terms of π.

16. For trapezoid *WXYZ*, explain how to find the length of $\overline{WZ}$.

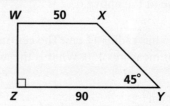

Name _____ Class _____ Date _____

Chapter Practice
Chapter 8

For Exercises 1–12, choose the correct letter.

1. How can you prove $\triangle ABC \sim \triangle FEG$?

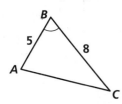

A AA ~ Postulate   B SSS ~ Theorem

C SAS ~ Theorem   D ASA ~ Theorem

E none of the above

2. $\triangle XYZ \sim \triangle RST$. What can you conclude?

A $XY = RS$ B $m\angle X = m\angle Y$

C $m\angle S = m\angle Y$ D $\triangle XYZ \cong \triangle RST$

E none of the above

3. Find the value of x.

A 6   B 4

C $\frac{3}{4}$ D $\frac{144}{3}$

E none of the above

4. Two similar triangles have perimeters in ratio $5:3$. What is the ratio of their areas?

A $5:3$ B $5:1$ C $25:9$ D $125:27$

E none of the above

5. Find the value of x.

A $\frac{28}{5}$ B $\frac{20}{7}$

C 6   D $\frac{35}{4}$

E none of the above

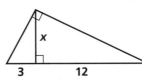

6. Find the value of x.

A 10   B $\frac{20}{3}$

C 15   D $\frac{48}{5}$

E none of the above

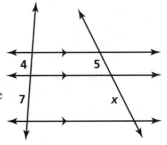

7. In which figure can you conclude that the triangles are similar?

I. .

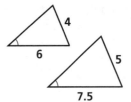

II.

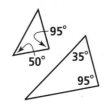

III.

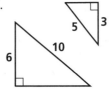

A I and II   B I and III   C II and III

D I, II and III   E none of the above

8. Find the value of x.

A 25

B $\frac{200}{9}$

C 21

D 22

E none of the above

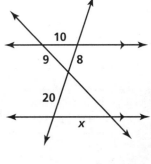

9. If $\frac{x}{y} = \frac{m}{p}$, what can you conclude?

A $xy = mp$ B $\frac{x}{p} = \frac{m}{y}$ C $xm = py$

D $\frac{p}{y} = \frac{m}{x}$ E none of the above

10. Find the value of x.

A $\frac{15}{4}$ B $\frac{12}{5}$

C $\frac{20}{3}$ D 2

E none of the above

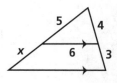

11. Find the value of *x*.

A 8   **B** $2\sqrt{5}$

C $4\sqrt{5}$ **D** $16\sqrt{5}$

E none of the above

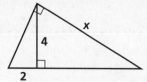

12. In the figure to the right, what can you conclude?

A $YM = ZM$

B $m\angle Y = m\angle XMZ$

C $m\angle Z = m\angle XMZ$

D $(XY)(ZM) = (XZ)(YM)$

E none of the above

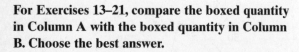

For Exercises 13–21, compare the boxed quantity in Column A with the boxed quantity in Column B. Choose the best answer.

A The quantity in Column A is greater.

B The quantity in Column B is greater.

C The two quantities are equal.

D The relationship cannot be determined on the basis of the information supplied.

Column A	Column B

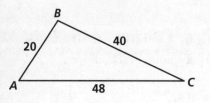

13. $\dfrac{AB}{RS}$ $\dfrac{AC}{RT}$

14. similarity ratio of $\triangle ABC$ to $\triangle RST$ RS

$\triangle LMN \sim \triangle L'M'N'$

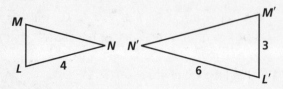

15. $m\angle L$ $m\angle L'$

Column A	**Column B**

16. LM similarity ratio of $\triangle LMN$ to $\triangle L'M'N'$

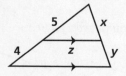

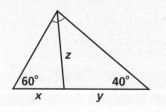

17. x y

18. z y

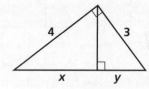

19. x y

20. z y

21. x y

For Exercises 22–24, write your answer.

22. **Open-Ended** Sketch a pair of similar scalene triangles with similarity ratio $3 : 2$.

23. **Writing** Explain why you can conclude that any two isosceles triangles with a vertex angle of 40° must be similar.

24. A tree casts a shadow 40 ft long. A man who is 6 ft tall stands nearby and casts a shadow 9 ft long. Find the height of the tree.

Name _____ Class _____ Date _____

Chapter Practice

Chapter 9

For Exercises 1–7, choose the correct letter.

1. Which of the following is equivalent to the number line graph?

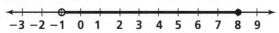

- **A** t is greater than -1 or less than 8.
- **B** t is between -1 and 8.
- **C** t is greater than -1 and less than 8.
- **D** t is less than or equal to 8 and greater than -1.
- **E** none of the above

2. Which sentence contains enough information to describe a vector?

- **A** A hiker walks 12 mi.
- **B** A car travels southeast at 50 mi/h.
- **C** An airplane travels at 600 mi/h.
- **D** A fish swims upstream.
- **E** none of the above

3. Which of the following statements is *not* true for the equation $4x + 3y = 15$?

- **A** The y-intercept is 5.
- **B** The line has a positive slope.
- **C** The x-intercept is 3.75.
- **D** The line contains the point $(3, 1)$.
- **E** none of the above

4. Find the value of x.

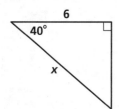

- **A** 4.6
- **B** 7.2
- **C** 7.8
- **D** 9.3
- **E** 10

5. Express tan B as a ratio.

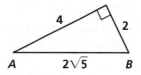

- **A** $\dfrac{1}{2}$
- **B** 2
- **C** $\dfrac{\sqrt{5}}{10}$
- **D** $\dfrac{\sqrt{5}}{5}$

6. A meteorologist measures the angle of elevation of a weather balloon as 35°. The balloon is 1500 m from her location. How high is the balloon above the ground?

- **A** 1500 sin 35
- **B** 1500 cos 35
- **C** $\dfrac{1500}{\sin 35}$
- **D** $\dfrac{1500}{\cos 35}$

7. Which describes the vector in ordered pair notation?

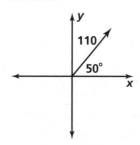

- **A** $\langle 84.3, 70.7 \rangle$
- **B** $\langle 63.5, 59.1 \rangle$
- **C** $\langle 70.7, 84.3 \rangle$
- **D** $\langle 59.1, 63.5 \rangle$

For Exercises 8–12, compare the boxed quantity in Column A with the boxed quantity in Column B. Choose the best answer.

A The quantity in Column A is greater.

B The quantity in Column B is greater.

C The two quantities are equal.

D The relationship cannot be determined on the basis of the information supplied.

| Column A | Column B |

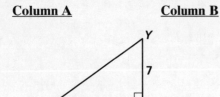

8. | $\sin X$ | $\cos X$ |

9. | $3 - (\frac{2}{3} \cdot 6)$ | $(3 - \frac{2}{3}) \cdot 6$ |

10. | area of a hexagon with apothem $2\sqrt{3}$ | area of an equilateral triangle with apothem $2\sqrt{2}$ |

11. | $3x$ | $4x$ |

12. | the magnitude of a_W$\langle -5, 2 \rangle$ | the magnitude of b_W$\langle 3, 3 \rangle$ |

For Exercises 13–17, write your answer.

13. Find the area of a regular dodecagon with side length 14. Express your answer in terms of trigonometric ratios.

14. A bug standing at the origin of the *x-y* plane begins walking north. After *a* units, the bug turns and walks *b* units east. Finally it walks *c* units south. Draw the vector describing the bug's final position and give the coordinates.

15. What is the probability that a letter of the alphabet picked at random is a vowel: A, E, I, O, or U?

16. A surveyor measuring the height of a tree stands 100 ft from it. Her angle-measuring device is 5 ft above the ground. The angle of elevation to the top of the tree is 52°. How tall is the tree to the nearest foot?

17. Find *x*. Round to the nearest tenth.

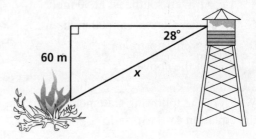

Name_____ Class_____ Date_____

Chapter Practice

Chapter 10

For Exercises 1–12, choose the correct letter.

1. Which of the following equations is *not* equivalent to the others?

   A $7 = n$ **B** $3n + 1 = 22$

   C $\frac{n}{7} = 1$ **D** $2n = 14$

   E $\frac{n}{2} = \frac{14}{2}$

2. Which of the following is true?

   A $5^0 = 0$ **B** $\frac{1}{5^0} = \frac{1}{5}$

   C $\frac{x^6}{x^2} = x^3$ **D** $(2x)^4 = 8x^4$

   E none of the above

3. Two similar cones have surface areas of 12π in.^{2} and 27π in.^{2}. The volume of the smaller cone is 16π in.^{3}. Find the volume of the larger cone.

   A 21π in.^{3} **B** 24π in.^{3} **C** 36π in.^{3}

   D 91.125 in.^{3} **E** none of the above

4. What is the volume of a regular square pyramid with base 6 cm and height 7 cm?

   A 84 cm^3 **B** 98 cm^3 **C** 252 cm^3

   D 56 cm^3 **E** none of the above

5. The area of a net of a cube is 150 cm^2. What is the length of an edge of the cube?

   A 5 cm   **B** 10 cm   **C** 15 cm   **D** 25 cm

   E none of the above

6. If the radius and height of a cylinder are doubled, then its lateral area

   A stays the same   **B** doubles

   C triples   **D** quadruples

   E none of the above

7. Find the volume of the prism.

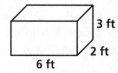

   A 36 ft^2 **B** 18 ft^2

   C 18 ft^3 **D** 36 ft^3

   E none of the above

8. A sphere has a radius of 6 ft. Which of the following space figures has a volume equal to the sphere's?

   A a cube with an edge of 6 ft

   B a cylinder with a radius of 4 ft and a height of 18 ft

   C a pyramid with a base of 120 ft^2 and a height of 10 ft

   D a cone with a radius of 6 ft and a height of 10 ft

   E none of the above

9. A pencil has a length of 17 cm and a diameter of 0.7 cm. The pencil's lead core has a diameter of 0.3 cm. What is the volume of the wooden portion of the pencil to the nearest whole number?

   A 21 cm^3 **B** 6 cm^3 **C** 5 cm^3

   D 2 cm^3 **E** 1 cm^3

10. Which space figures can you use to describe the shape of the old-fashioned gumball machine?

   Use diagram for Exercises 10 and 11.

     I. prism
     II. cylinder
     III. sphere
     IV. cone

   (6 in., 5 in., 3 in., 7 in.)

   A I and II   **B** I and III

   C I, III, and IV   **D** I, II, and III

   E none of the above

11. Find the volume of the entire gumball machine to the nearest tenth.

   A 105.0 in.^{3} **B** 1009.8 in.^{3}

   C 904.8 in.^{3} **D** 1234.6 in.^{3}

   E none of the above

12. A sphere's surface area is 144π m^2.
Find its volume.

    A 48π m^3 **B** 288π m^3 **C** $2{,}304\pi$ m^3

    D $18{,}432\pi$ m^3 **E** none of the above

For Exercises 13–15, compare the boxed quantity in Column A with the boxed quantity in Column B. Choose the best answer.

    A The quantity in Column A is greater.

    B The quantity in Column B is greater.

    C The two quantities are equal.

    D The relationship cannot be determined on the basis of the information supplied.

Column A   **Column B**

13.

surface area of sphere X	the sum of the surface areas of spheres Y and Z

14.

$4x^2$	$(-2x)^2$

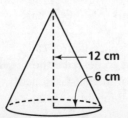

15.

the volume of the cone	half the volume of a cylinder with the same radius and height

For Exercises 16–21, write your answer.

16. A cylindrical compact disk carrying case has a volume of 1360 cm^3. A single compact disk has a diameter of 12 cm and is 1.2 mm thick. If compact disks fit snugly into this carrying case, how many CDs can the case hold?

17. **Open-ended** Draw two different dartboards. Shade regions of each board. Then determine for each board the probability that a randomly thrown dart that hits the board will land in its shaded area.

18. **Writing** At the local movie theater, beverages are sold in cylindrical containers. A small drink has a diameter of 3.5 in. and a height of 8 in. A medium drink has a diameter of 5 in. and a height of 8 in. For a double feature special, the theatre is offering two small beverages for the price of one medium beverage. Is this a good deal? Explain.

19. If the ratio of the surface areas of two similar prisms is $\frac{49}{81}$, what is the ratio of their volumes?

20. **Open-ended** Create a foundation drawing for a structure composed of 6 cubes. Then, based on your foundation plan, create an isometric drawing and an orthographic drawing.

21. Draw a net for the box. Label the net with the appropriate dimensions.

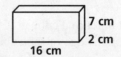

Chapter Practice

Chapter 11

For Exercises 1–15, choose the correct letter.

1. Find the equation of the circle with center $(3, 5)$ and radius of 4.

   A $(x + 3)^2 + (y + 5)^2 = 4$

   B $(x + 3)^2 + (y + 5)^2 = 16$

   C $(x - 3)^2 + (y - 5)^2 = 4$

   D $(x - 3)^2 + (y - 5)^2 = 16$

   E none of these

2. $\overline{AT}$ is tangent to the circle at point T. Find AT.

   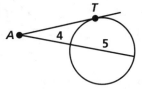

   A 6   **B** 4.5   **C** $\sqrt{20}$

   D 20   **E** none of these

3. A circle with center C has radius of 5. $CX = 3$. Find AB.

   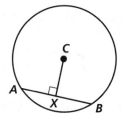

   A 4   **B** 6

   C 8   **D** 10

   E none of these

4. Find the value of x in $\odot O$.

   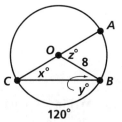

   A 60   **B** 30

   C 20   **D** 15

   E none of these

5. Find CB in $\odot O$.

   A 8   **B** 16   **C** $4\sqrt{3}$ **D** $8\sqrt{3}$

   E none of these

6. Find $m\angle BAC$.

   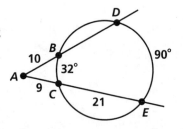

   A 58   **B** 32

   C 29   **D** 61

   E none of these

7. Find BD in the figure for Exercise 6.

   A 17   **B** 20   **C** 22   **D** 27

   E none of these

8. In circle O, if chords $\overline{AB}$ and $\overline{XY}$ are equidistant from O, what can you conclude?

   A $AB > OA$ **B** $AB < OA$

   C $AB = XY > OA$ **D** $AB = XY$

   E none of these

9. In the diagram to the right, $\overline{AB} \perp \overline{XY}$ and $\overline{AB}$ bisects $\overline{XY}$. What can you conclude?

   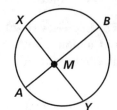

   A M is the center of the circle.

   B $\overline{XY}$ bisects $\overline{AB}$

   C $\overline{AB}$ passes through the center of the circle.

   D $XY = AB$

   E none of these

10. Find the value of x.

    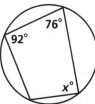

    A 88   **B** 92

    C 84   **D** 90

    E none of these

11. Find the center and radius of the circle $x^2 + (y + 3)^2 = 2$.

    A $C(0, 3); r = 2$ **B** $C(0, 3); r = 4$

    C $C(0, -3); r = 2$ **D** $C(0, -3); r = 4$

    E none of these

12. $\overline{PT}$ is tangent to $\odot O$ at T. Find the value of r.

    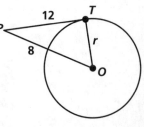

    A 4   **B** 5

    C 6   **D** 8

    E none of these

13. Find the value of x.

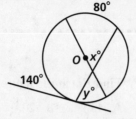

A 60   B 70
C 80   D 90
E none of these

14. Find the value of y.

A 50   B 60   C 70   D 110
E none of these

15. Find the radius of $\odot O$.

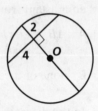

A 2   B 4
C 8   D $\sqrt{20}$
E none of these

For Exercises 16–20, compare the boxed quantity in Column A with the boxed quantity in Column B. Choose the best answer.

A The quantity in Column A is greater.

B The quantity in Column B is greater.

C The two quantities are equal.

D The relationship cannot be determined on the basis of the information supplied.

<u>Column A</u>   <u>Column B</u>

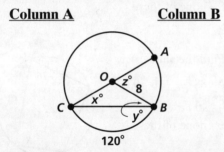

16. x y

17. x z

<u>Column A</u>   <u>Column B</u>

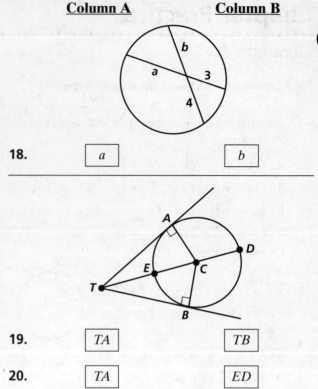

18. a b

19. TA TB

20. TA ED

For Exercises 21–23, write your answer.

21. **Open-ended** Sketch a circle containing congruent chords.

22. **Writing** Explain why you can conclude that $\triangle DAX \sim \triangle CBX$.

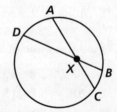

23. **Writing** A circle has diameter with endpoints $(1, 3)$ and $(3, -7)$. Explain why its equation is $(x - 2)^2 + (y + 2)^2 = 26$.

Chapter Practice

Chapter 12

For Exercises 1–11, choose the correct letter.

1. What type of symmetry does the letter V have?

   A rotational   **B** reflectional

   C point   **D** rotational and point

   E none of the above

2. What is the image of $(1, 2)$ rotated $90°$ about the origin?

   A $(2, 1)$ **B** $(-1, 22)$ **C** $(-2, -1)$

   D $(-2, 1)$ **E** none of the above

3. Which of the following is an irrational number?

   A $\sqrt{2}$ **B** 0.125 **C** $\frac{1}{3}$

   D 101 **E** none of the above

4. What is the image of $(6, 4)$ reflected in $x = 3$?

   A $(9, 4)$ **B** $(0, 4)$ **C** $(6, 2)$

   D $(4, 9)$ **E** none of the above

5. The point $(5, 1)$ is reflected in the x-axis then translated $<-6, 2>$. Where is its image?

   A first quadrant   **B** third quadrant

   C second quadrant   **D** fourth quadrant

   E none of the above

6. For art class, you have constructed a model of your family's car. If your model is 4 inches high and your car is 5 feet high, what scale factor did you use?

   A $\frac{4}{5}$ **B** $\frac{5}{4}$ **C** $\frac{1}{20}$ **D** $\frac{1}{15}$

   E none of the above

7. Which figure does not tessellate?

   A square   **B** isosceles trapezoid

   C pentagon   **D** hexagon

   E none of the above

8. Which figure does *not* have point symmetry?

   A a square   **B** a rectangle

   C a circle   **D** a 5-pointed star

   E none of the above

9. What is the angle between the mirrors for this kaleidescope image?

   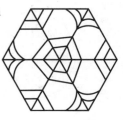

   A $15°$ **B** $30°$

   C $45°$ **D** $60°$

   E none of the above

10. Which clock face does *not* have rotational symmetry?

    A   **B**

    C   **D**

    E none of the above

11. If you reflect $\triangle TAR$ in the y-axis, what kind of quadrilateral is $TT'R'R$?

    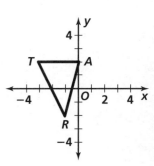

    A parallelogram

    B kite

    C rhombus

    D trapezoid

    E none of the above

For Exercises 12 and 13, compare the boxed quantity in Column A with the boxed quantity in Column B. Choose the best answer.

  A The quantity in Column A is greater.

  B The quantity in Column B is greater.

  C The two quantities are equal.

  D The relationship cannot be determined on the basis of the information supplied.

Column A	Column B
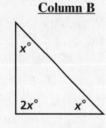	$x°$ ⟋ $2x°$ $x°$

12.

the angle between the mirrors	x

13.

number of lines of symmetry in a square	number of lines of symmetry in an isosceles trapezoid

For Exercises 14–17, write your answer.

14. A dime's diameter is about 1.7 cm. A quarter's diameter is approximately 2.4 cm. When a dime is placed on an overhead projector, its projected image appears to be much larger. If the overhead projector is not moved and the quarter is placed on it, the diameter of the quarter's image is 12 cm. Find the scale factor for the projected image of the dime.

15. A car is shown making a turn at an intersection. What kind of transformation is the car undergoing? Explain.

16. State whether each mapping is a reflection, rotation, translation, or glide reflection.

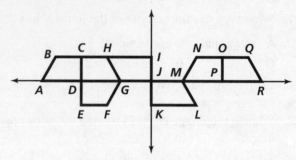

  a. ▱ *ABCD* → ▱ *GHCD*

  b. ▱ *HGJI* → ▱ *LMJK*

  c. ▱ *GFED* → ▱ *RQOP*

  d. ▱ *MNOP* → ▱ *ABCD*

17. Open-ended

  a. Draw a figure that has at least two lines of symmetry.

  b. Sketch its lines of symmetry.

  c. Use the figure to create a tessellation. Draw a three-column-by-three-row figure.

End-of-Course Test

1. A plane parallel to the base of a right cone intersects the cone. Which best describes the possible shape(s) of the intersection of the plane and the cone?

   A a circle or an ellipse

   B a circle or a triangle

   C a circle only

   D a circle or a point

2. Find the converse of "If it is a shovel, then it is a tool."

   A If it is a tool, then it is a shovel.

   B If it is not a shovel, then it is not a tool.

   C If it is a shovel, then it is not a tool.

   D If it is a tool, then it is not a shovel.

3. Find the contrapositive of the following statement. If a figure has four sides, it is a quadrilateral.

   A If a figure is a quadrilateral, it does not have four sides.

   B If a figure does not have four sides, it is a quadrilateral.

   C If a figure is not a quadrilateral, it does not have four sides.

   D If a figure has four sides, it is not a quadrilateral.

4. Which best describes the angles shown?

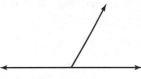

   A supplementary

   B complementary

   C corresponding

   D vertical

5. Given: All points on a circle with center C are equidistant from C, and points A and B are on a circle with center C. We conclude: Points A and B are equidistant from C. What type of reasoning did we employ?

   A deductive reasoning

   B inductive reasoning

   C converse reasoning

   D all of the above

6. Which of the following describes the figure below?

   A $\overline{YZ}$

   B $\overrightarrow{YZ}$

   C $\overleftrightarrow{YZ}$

   D $\overrightarrow{ZY}$

7. Which is a true statement?

A A rhombus is always a rectangle.

B A square is sometimes a rectangle and sometimes a rhombus, but not always both.

C A square is the only quadrilateral that is both a rhombus and a rectangle.

D No rhombus is a rectangle.

8. If $RS = 34.8$ and $QS = 81.6$, find QR.

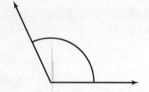

A 46.8

B 116.4

C 34.8

D 36.8

9. Estimate the measure of the angle.

A about 180°

B about 120°

C about 100°

D about 140°

10. Which of the following are coplanar?

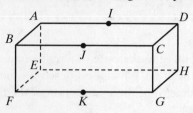

A H, D, C, E

B F, G, H, D

C A, B, C, G

D A, E, F, B

11. Classify the triangle with sides of length 23, 23, and 23.

A isosceles

B straight

C scalene

D equilateral

12. In the figure shown, $\overleftrightarrow{HC} \| \overleftrightarrow{GD}$ and $m\angle ABC = 150°$. Which of the following statements is *false*?

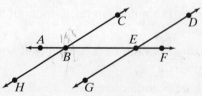

A $\angle ABC$ and $\angle AED$ are corresponding angles.

B $m\angle GEF = 30°$

C $\angle ABH$ and $\angle AEG$ are corresponding angles.

D $m\angle DEF = 30°$

13. Find the word or words that best complete the sentence.

Two lines that lie in parallel planes _____ intersect.

A always

B sometimes

C never

D not enough information to tell

14. Find the values of x, y, and z.

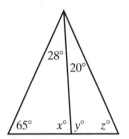

A $x = 87, y = 93, z = 48$

B $x = 93, y = 87, z = 48$

C $x = 87, y = 93, z = 67$

D $x = 93, y = 87, z = 67$

15. Find the measure of one of the interior angles of a regular polygon with ten sides.

A $144°$

B $36°$

C $18°$

D $162°$

16. Refer to the figure shown. Given $\overline{TV} \cong \overline{VW}$ and $\overline{UV} \cong \overline{VX}$, which of the following statements is true?

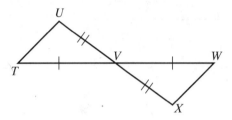

A $\triangle TUV \cong \triangle WXV$ by ASA.

B $\triangle TUV \cong \triangle VWX$ by SAS.

C $\triangle TUV \cong \triangle WXV$ by SAS.

D $\triangle TUV \cong \triangle XWV$ by ASA.

17. In which of the following could you efficiently prove △1 ≅ △2 using the HL Theorem?

I.

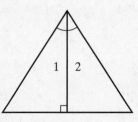

II.

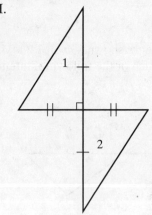

III.

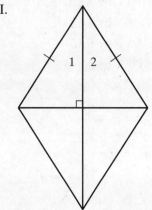

A II only

B I only

C II and III

D III only

18. If △ABC ≅ △DEF, AB = 3 cm, m∠ABC = 19° and m∠DFE = 53°, which of the following statements is *false*?

A $\overline{BC} \cong \overline{EF}$

B FD = 3 cm

C ∠D ≅ ∠A

D m∠CAB= 108°

19. One side of a parallelogram has a length of 1.4 feet while another side has a length of 36.3 feet. What is the perimeter of the parallelogram?

A 39.1 ft

B 50.82 ft

C 75.4 ft

D 37.7 ft

20. Find the measures of the numbered angles in the parallelogram.

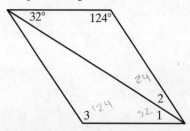

A m∠1= 32°; m∠2= 24°; m∠3= 124°

B m∠1= 24°; m∠2= 32°; m∠3= 124°

C m∠1= 16°; m∠2= 62°; m∠3= 148°

D m∠1= 32°; m∠2= 16°; m∠3= 148°

21. In rhombus $ABCD$, $AB = 13$ and $AC = 16$. Find BD to the nearest tenth.

A 20.5

B 28.8

C 18.2

D 18.7

22. What is the value of x?

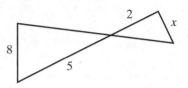

A 3.25

B 2

C 5

D cannot be determined

23. Dawn is laying computer cables in the ceiling of a large building. A 75-ft cable to office B1 and a 100-ft cable to office B2 meet at a right angle. Offices B1 and B2 are both on the same outer wall of the building. If Dawn lays one cable from where the first two cables meet directly to the outer wall, how far will it be from there to office B1?

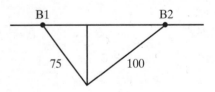

A 62 ft

B 56 ft

C 45 ft

D 125 ft

24. The triangles below are similar. Find the length of x.

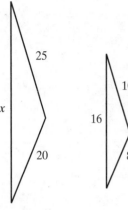

A 40

B 6.4

C 42.5

D 42

25. Triangles ABC and XYZ are similar with $\angle A \cong \angle X$, and $\angle B \cong \angle Y$. If AB, BC, and AC are 10 inches, 12 inches, and 13 inches, respectively, and XY is 14 inches, find XZ. (Answer to the nearest tenth.)

A 16.8 in.

B 8.6 in.

C 18.2 in.

D 9.3 in.

26. In $\triangle ABC$, J is on $\overline{AB}$, K is on $\overline{BC}$, and $\overline{JK} \parallel \overline{AC}$. Solve for x if $JB = 7$, $AJ = 18$, $BK = x + 3$, and $KC = 5x$.

A 30

B $\dfrac{17}{54}$

C $\dfrac{54}{17}$

D $\dfrac{1}{30}$

27. The area of a regular octagon is 25 cm^2. What is the area of a regular octagon with sides six times as large?

A 900 cm^2

B 3750 cm^2

C 835 cm^2

D 150 cm^2

28. Find the measure, to the nearest tenth, of the diagonal of a rectangle with dimensions 17 cm by 4 cm.

A 16.5 cm

B 4.6 cm

C 16.4 cm

D 17.5 cm

29. A radio station is going to construct a 12-foot tower for a new antenna. The tower will be supported by 3 cables. One end of each cable is attached to the top of the tower; the other end of each is attached to the ground 16 feet from the base of the tower. Find the total length of the three cables.

A 100 ft

B 60 ft

C 20 ft

D 80 ft

30. In $\triangle ABC$, $\angle A$ is a right angle and $m\angle B = 45°$. If $AB = 33$ feet, find AC.

A 33 ft

B 46.669 ft

C 28.579 ft

D 57.158 ft

31. Which of the following *cannot* be the lengths of a 30°-60°-90° triangle?

A $\dfrac{9}{2}, 9, \dfrac{9}{2}\sqrt{3}$

B $8, 16, 8\sqrt{3}$

C $\dfrac{4}{3}, \dfrac{8}{3}, \dfrac{4}{3}\sqrt{3}$

D $5, \dfrac{5}{2}, 5\sqrt{3}$

32. Use the diagram to find cos x as a fraction in simplest form.

A $\frac{4}{5}$

B $1\frac{1}{3}$

C $\frac{3}{4}$

D $\frac{3}{5}$

33. $\overline{AD}$ is tangent to both circles in the figure (not drawn to scale). If $BA = 8$, $AD = 25$, and $CD = 15$, find the length of $\overline{BC}$ to the nearest tenth.

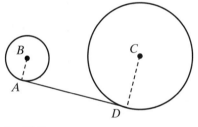

A 26.0

B 16.6

C 26.2

D 35.4

34. The circle is inscribed in the pentagon as shown (not drawn to scale). If $QZ = 11$, $YX = 6$, $XW = 10$, $UW = 20$, and $SU = 13$, find the perimeter of the pentagon.

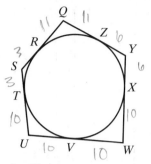

A 80

B 120

C 115

D 85

35. Given: In $\odot O$, $m\widehat{BAC} = 298°$. Find $m\angle A$.

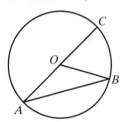

A 31°

B 15.5°

C 25°

D 12.5°

36. A chord 18 cm long contains the center of circle *O*. What is the radius of the circle to the nearest tenth?

   A   not enough information provided

   B   28.3 cm

   C   18.0 cm

   D   9.0 cm

37. A solar energy collector needs several 3 in. by 3 in. square panels to cover a rectangular area 17 ft by 5 ft. How many of the square panels are needed?

   A   113

   B   765

   C   1360

   D   4080

38. Find the circumference of a circle whose radius is 8 inches. (Use $\pi \approx 3.14$)

   A   50.24 in.

   B   0.785 in.

   C   0.393 in.

   D   25.12 in.

39. For a circle of radius 8 feet, find the arc length of a central angle of 6°.

   A $\frac{4}{5}\pi$ feet

   B 48π feet

   C $\frac{8}{15}\pi$ feet

   D $\frac{4}{15}\pi$ feet

40. Find the area:

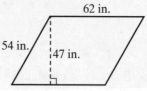

   A   3348 in.^{2}

   B   3131 in.^{2}

   C   2726 in.^{2}

   D   2914 in.^{2}

41. Compare the quantity in Column A with the quantity in Column B.

Column A	Column B
the area of a regular octagon with apothem 4 and side 4	the area of a regular hexagon with apothem 4 and side 4

   A   The quantity in Column A is greater.

   B   The quantity in Column B is greater.

   C   The two quantities are equal.

   D   The relationship cannot be determined on the basis of the information given.

Name _____ Class _____ Date _____

42. Find the area of the shaded region. Use 3.14 for π.

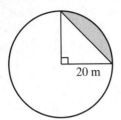

20 m

- **A** 314 m²
- **B** 428 m²
- **C** 114 m²
- **D** 200 m²

43. Which property justifies that $3(x - 4)$ is equivalent to $3x - 12$?

- **A** associative property
- **B** commutative property
- **C** distributive property
- **D** identity property

44. A rectangular prism is 12 cm long, 8 cm wide, and 6 cm high. Find the surface area of the prism.

- **A** 432 cm²
- **B** 576 cm²
- **C** 52 cm²
- **D** 26 cm²

45. Find the surface area of the cylinder to the nearest square unit. (Use Use $\pi \approx 3.14$)

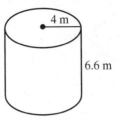

4 m

6.6 m

- **A** 42 m²
- **B** 266 m²
- **C** 26 m²
- **D** 133 m²

46. The pyramid shown has a rectangular base and faces that are isosceles triangles. Which measure BEST approximates the total surface area?

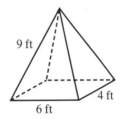

9 ft

6 ft

4 ft

- **A** 114.0 ft²
- **B** 72.0 ft²
- **C** 407.3 ft²
- **D** 110.0 ft²

47. Find the surface area of a sphere that has a diameter of 10 centimeters. Use 3.14 for π and round your answer to the nearest centimeter.

- **A** 4187 cm²
- **B** 523 cm²
- **C** 314 cm²
- **D** 1256 cm²

48. Find the volume of the triangular prism.

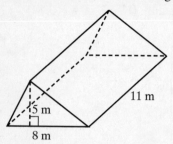

11 m

5 m

8 m

A 440 m^3

B 31 m^3

C 220 m^3

D 51 m^3

49. Find the volume of the cone that has a diameter of 6 feet and a height of 16 feet. (Use 3.14 for π.)

A 452.16 ft^3

B 150.72 ft^3

C 301.44 ft^3

D 602.88 ft^3

50. Which best describes the angles shown?

A supplementary

B complementary

C corresponding

D vertical

51. A design on a balloon is 2 cm wide when the balloon holds 62 cm^3 of air. How much must the balloon hold for the design to be 8 cm wide?

A 992 cm^3

B 3968 cm^3

C 248 cm^3

D 3879 cm^3

52. The dotted triangle is the image of the solid triangle. What is the scale factor?

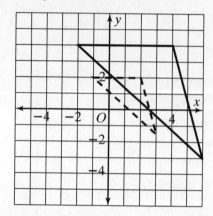

A 2

B $\frac{1}{2}$

C 4

D 3

53. Which of the following capital letters (if written simply) has at least one line of reflectional symmetry?

A J

B P

C H

D N

Name_____ Class_____ Date_____

54. Which graph represents a translation?

A
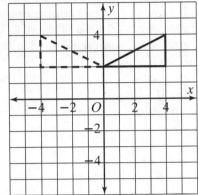

B
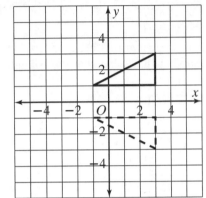

C
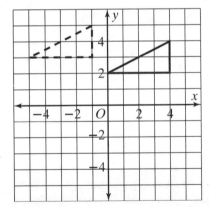

D
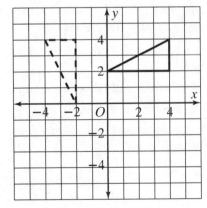

55. Find the distance between points $P(1, -2)$ and $Q(0, 2)$.

A $\sqrt{15}$
B $\sqrt{17}$
C $\sqrt{13}$
D $\sqrt{5}$

56. Find the coordinates of the midpoint of the segment connecting $H(5, -1)$ and $K(-9, 13)$.

A $(-2, 6)$
B $(14, 14)$
C $(7, 7)$
D $(-4, 12)$

57. Which net represents the surfaces of a triangular prism?

A
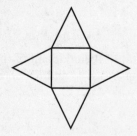

B
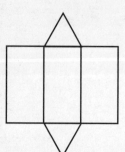

C
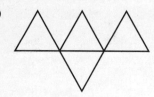

D

58. To find the height of a pole, a surveyor moves 50 meters away from the base of the pole and then, with a transit 2 meters tall, measures the angle of elevation to the top of the pole to be 63°. What is the height of the pole? Round your answer to the nearest meter.

A 98 m

B 25 m

C 27 m

D 100 m

59. If a dart is thrown at the target shown, what is the probability that it lands in the triangle?

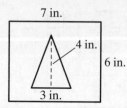

A $\frac{1}{2}$

B $\frac{5}{7}$

C $\frac{1}{7}$

D 1

60. Willson Avenue is perpendicular to both Babcock Street and Olive Street. Make a conclusion about the relationship between Babcock Street and Olive Street.

A Babcock Street and Olive Street are perpendicular.

B Babcock Street and Olive Street are parallel.

C Babcock Street and Olive Street intersect.

D Babcock Street and Olive Street form an acute angle.

SAT/ACT: Introduction

Each year, as a key step in their advancement toward college, more than two million high school students take the Scholastic Assessment Test (SAT I)[1] and the American College Test (ACT).[2] Many also take the more modest counterparts of these tests, the Preliminary Scholastic Assessment Test (PSAT/NMSQT)[1] and the Preliminary American College Test, now known as PLAN.[2]

Experts disagree as to how well the SAT I and the ACT predict college performance. However fair or unfair it may be, most colleges base their decisions on whether or not to accept a student, at least to some degree, on the student's SAT I or ACT score. (PSAT/NMSQT scores are used to qualify students for National Merit Scholarships. Most students take the PSAT/NMSQT and PLAN, however, as practice for the SAT I and ACT.) In general, the larger the college, the more importance it places on SAT I or ACT test scores in assessing its applicants. Also, the more demanding a college's academic standards, the higher the test scores it expects of its applicants.

Whichever colleges you apply to, your high school transcript and activities, your college application form and supporting materials, and often letters of recommendation and personal interviews will have the greatest influence on whether you are accepted. Still, it's to your advantage to achieve the highest score that you can on the SAT I or ACT. This section was designed in three parts to help you meet that goal on the math portions of the two tests.

The first part will tell you what you need to know about the two tests so that you won't be surprised when you sit down on test day and open your booklet. The second part will provide you with a host of test-taking tips. The third part is an SAT /ACT Practice Test you can take to apply what you've learned. If you feel you need more work with specific math content, you can turn to your textbook for a more comprehensive discussion of the relevant mathematics or for extra practice.

In the weeks leading up to whichever test you plan to take, you should spend a set amount of time each day preparing for it. Review key math topics, familiarize yourself with the test formats, and practice the test-taking skills described in this book. Of course, there's no telling how much your preparations will improve your score. Given the importance of the results, however, you have nothing to lose in preparing yourself fully for the test, and a great deal to gain.

[1] SAT is a registered trademark of, and the PSAT is a trademark owned by, the College Entrance Examination Board, which was not involved in the production of, and does not endorse, this product.

[2] ACT Assessment and the PLAN are registered trademarks owned by ACT, Inc., which was not involved in the production of, and does not endorse, this product.

SAT/ACT: Highlights

The SAT I and PSAT/NMSQT

The SAT I takes three hours. There are three sections in the math portion of the test.

Section	Length	Number of Questions	Type of Question
I	30 minutes	25	Multiple-Choice
II	30 minutes	15	Quantitative Comparison
		10	Grid-ins
III	15 minutes	10	Multiple-Choice
Total	75 minutes	60	

The three question types (multiple-choice, quantitative comparison, and grid-ins) will be described later.

In each math section of the test, questions increase gradually in difficulty, with relatively easy questions in the first third of the section and relatively hard ones in the last third.

In addition to the sections listed above, there is a 30-minute "experimental" section, containing new SAT I math or verbal questions that are being tried out. This section is not scored.

The PSAT/NMSQT is similar to the SAT I, except that it lasts for only two hours. In the math portion of the PSAT/NMSQT, the SAT I's fifteen-minute, ten-question section is left out. There is no experimental section.

Both tests covers basic knowledge of arithmetic, algebra, and geometry. You are not expected to know the fine details of math. Naturally, the more you know, the more likely you are to do well in the test. The SAT I and PSAT/NMSQT, however, emphasize math reasoning and problem solving rather than comprehensive proficiency in mathematics.

The quadratic formula is one example of a fine detail. Neither the SAT I nor the PSAT/NMSQT requires you to know it. To solve quadratic equations on the tests, you can use factoring or other elementary methods. Of course, if you *do* know the quadratic formula, you might find it useful, either to solve a problem or to check an answer. In general, however, you're better off using logic and clear reasoning to solve problems, rather than advanced mathematics.

You're allowed to bring a calculator to either test—in fact, you're encouraged to do so. None of the questions will *require* the use of a calculator. On the average, however, students who use calculators wisely do slightly better than students who do not use them at all, and considerably better than students who use them unwisely. Wise use of the calculator will be discussed later.

SAT/ACT: Highlights

Scoring

Multiple-choice and quantitative comparison questions are scored the same way: you receive one point for a correct answer and no points if you leave an answer blank. If you answer incorrectly, there's a penalty:

- one-fourth of a point is subtracted from your score if the question has five answer choices;

- one-third of a point is subtracted from your score if the question has four answer choices.

With grid-ins, you receive one point for a correct answer and no points for an incorrect or blank answer.

Here's how one SAT I test was scored:

50 multiple-choice and quantitative comparison questions

28 correct	=	28 points
12 incorrect (5 answer choices)	=	$(-)$ 3 points $\quad(12 \times \frac{1}{4} = 3)$
7 incorrect (4 answer choices)	=	$(-)$ $2\frac{1}{3}$ points $\quad(7 \times \frac{1}{3} = 2\frac{1}{3})$
3 blank	=	0 points

10 grid-in questions

6 correct	=	6 points
3 incorrect	=	0 points
1 blank	=	0 points
Raw Score	=	**$28\frac{2}{3}$ points**

The policy of subtracting a fraction of a point for incorrect answers on multiple-choice and quantitative comparison questions is called a "guessing penalty." However, as you'll learn in the part on test-taking tips, there's a way you can turn this so-called penalty to your advantage.

The raw score is now rounded to the nearest point and converted to a "scaled" score between 200 and 800 (SAT I), or 20 and 80 (PSAT/NMSQT). There are no passing or failing scores.

About a month after you take either test, you'll receive your results. These consist of your scaled score and a "percentile" score. The percentile score allows you to compare your results with those of all the other students who took the test. A score in the 64th percentile means that you did better than 64 percent of the people who took the test. The average SAT I math score nationwide is 500 points.

SAT/ACT: Highlights

Question Types

There are three types of questions on the math section of the SAT I.

Multiple-Choice Questions

Five answers are given for each multiple-choice question. Decide on the correct choice and fill in the corresponding oval on the answer sheet.

If 2 cans of tomatoes weigh 28 ounces, what is the weight, in ounces, of 7 cans of tomatoes?

(A) 2   (B) 8   (C) 56   (D) 98   (E) 196   Ⓐ Ⓑ Ⓒ ● Ⓔ

Quantitative Comparison Questions

In quantitative comparison questions, you are given two boxed quantities, one in Column A and one in Column B. You must compare the two quantities. On your answer sheet, fill in oval

- A if the quantity in Column A is greater;
- B if the quantity in Column B is greater;
- C if the two quantities are equal;
- D if you cannot determine which quantity is greater.

An E response is not scored. If two of the three relationships (A, B, or C) can be true, choose D.

Column A | Column B
$$2^3$$ | $$3^2$$ Ⓐ ● Ⓒ Ⓓ Ⓔ

Information relevant to both boxed quantities is centered above them and not boxed.

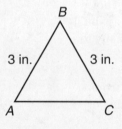

| AB | | AC | Ⓐ Ⓑ Ⓒ ● Ⓔ

Grid-in Questions

Grid-in questions are called "student-produced responses" on the test. Each requires you to calculate the correct answer to a question and then write it on the answer grid. Gridding an answer incorrectly will result in a zero score even if your answer is correct. For that reason, you should review the method for gridding answers *before* you take the test, because there are several ways to grid incorrectly. The following pages will give you a chance to do that.

SAT/ACT PREPARATION

SAT/ACT: Highlights

Sample Grids

Your responses are recorded on a special answer grid that provides ways of showing decimal points and fraction bars. You will be able to code decimal and fraction answers. For example, a student who gets an answer of 23.9 on a problem would code the answer as shown in this grid.

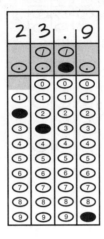

The grid is composed of four columns. If you look closely, you will notice that along with the digits 0 through 9, the division sign (/) and the decimal point (.) are available. *The first column cannot be filled with 0 or /.* Also, each character in the answer must occupy a single column in the grid. So the answer 23.9 requires all four available columns. Notice that there is no provision in the grid structure for coding negative values. *This is a clear message that there will be no questions in this part of the test that have negative answers.*

The following guidelines and grids illustrate how to code decimals, fractions, and mixed-number answers on this section of the book.

Each answer is shown with more than one coded grid. The grids show that the format is quite flexible. The examples should also make you realize that you may need to rewrite an answer in an equivalent form in order to code it correctly on the grid.

Grid-Coding Guidelines

Code: 0.65341

1. **Complete Answers** If a decimal answer cannot be fully coded, the coded answer must be as complete as possible.

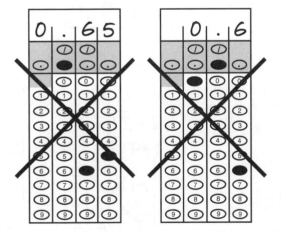

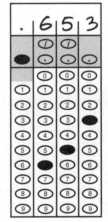

SAT/ACT: Highlights

Code: $\frac{5}{9}$

2. **Coding** There is a maximum of four columns on each grid. Each digit, decimal point, or division sign must occupy its own column. Coding may begin in any column as long as the answer is complete as described above. Do not leave a blank column between two marked columns. The scoring machine does not read the numbers above the columns, but writing the answer there may help you code correctly.

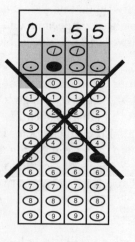
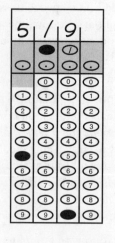
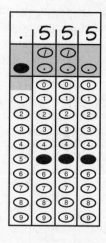

Code: $\frac{7}{5}$

3. **Improper Fractions** Improper fractions such as $\frac{23}{6}$ and $\frac{81}{9}$ may be coded directly. Other improper fractions, such as $\frac{150}{60}$, must be reduced or rewritten as an equivalent decimal in order to fit into the four available columns.

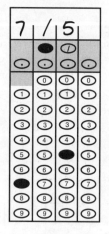

Code: $2\frac{2}{3}$

4. **Mixed Numbers** Mixed numbers must be rewritten as improper fractions or decimals. For $2\frac{2}{3}$, completing the grid with

| 2 | 2 | / | |

is not a correct option since it would be read as $\frac{22}{3}$.

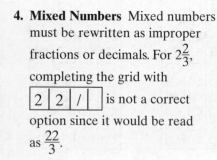

SAT/ACT: Highlights

Code: $\frac{1}{5} < x < \frac{1}{4}$

5. **Multiple Correct Answers** Some questions may have many correct answers. If any number x such that $0.2 < x < 0.25$ satisfies the problem, then any answer from the set of {0.201, 0.202, …, 0.248, 0.249} would be scored as correct. Correct answers would also include fractional equivalents like $\frac{9}{40}$.

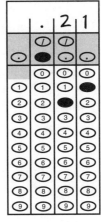 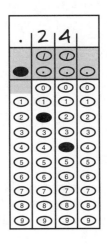 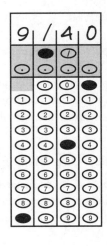

Code: 3.016

6. **Rounding Answers** A decimal answer does not need to be rounded unless explicit directions are given in the question.

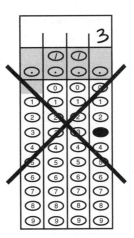 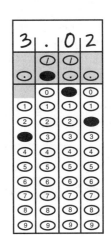

Code: $\frac{156}{6}$

7. **Simplifying Fractions** Simplifying is not required unless a fraction does not fit into the columns of the grid.

SAT/ACT: Highlights

Your high-school counselor can give information from the College Board to help you prepare for the **SAT I**. You can also learn more about the SAT I on the Web. The place to start is

http://www.collegeboard.org

where you will find current information from the test developers. There are also online daily practice questions, information about ways to prepare for the test, registration procedures, and lots about the ways tests are used by colleges.

The ACT and PLAN

The ACT takes three and one-half hours. The math section of the test lasts one hour and consists of 60 multiple-choice questions. Questions are arranged roughly in order of difficulty, from easiest to hardest. As with the SAT I, you may use a calculator on the ACT.

Scoring

Unlike the SAT I, the ACT is not scored by deducting a fraction of your incorrect answers from your correct ones. You get one point for a correct answer and no points for either an incorrect answer or an answer left blank. There is no penalty for guessing.

Here's how one ACT test was scored:

60 multiple-choice questions		
38 correct	=	38 points
22 incorrect	=	0 points
Raw Score	=	**38 points**

The content of ACT test questions is invariable. There are always

- 24 questions on pre-algebra and elementary algebra;
- 18 questions on intermediate algebra and coordinate geometry;
- 14 questions on geometry;
- 4 questions on basic trigonometry.

The PLAN is a mini-ACT. The math section of the test lasts 40 minutes and consists of 40 multiple-choice questions, apportioned as follows:

- 14 questions on pre-algebra;
- 8 questions on elementary algebra;
- 7 questions on coordinate geometry;
- 11 questions on plane geometry.

As on the ACT, you can use a calculator when you take the PLAN.

SAT/ACT: Highlights

Getting Your Results

You'll receive your ACT results in four to six weeks. Your math score (and your score in each of the other three areas of the test) will be a number from 1 to 36; 36 will be the highest possible score. (The PLAN is scored from 1 to 32.) As with the SAT I, you'll also receive a percentile ranking so that you can compare your results with those of other students who took the test.

When to Take the ACT

The ACT is given several times each year. If possible, arrange to take the test on a day when "Test Information Release" is in effect. Following the test, for a small fee, you can receive a copy of the test that you took and a photocopy of your answer sheet.

Having survived the test somehow, you may find the suggestion that you revisit it through a copy of your very own answer sheet rather humorous. Nevertheless, there are distinct advantages to doing so. You can check to make sure the scoring machine didn't make any errors. More important, you can check your work to discover areas where you were strong and other areas where you need to "bone up" on the subject matter covered by the test. Such knowledge will be useful to you generally, and even more so if you decide to take the test again.

If you do take the ACT several times, you'll be allowed to decide which of your scores should be reported to colleges.

Your high-school counselor can also give you information from the American College Testing Program to help you prepare for the **ACT Assessment**. The ACT Web site as of this writing is

http://www.act.org

where you can learn more. When you register for the test, the American College Testing Program provides you with detailed information about the test. Their address is P.O. Box 168, Iowa City, Iowa 52240.

SAT/ACT: Test-Taking Tips

Preparing for the Test

Long-term planning for both the SAT I and the ACT should include the following:

Work hard in math class.

No amount of last-minute cramming can substitute for serious study in your current math class. Students who do well in their math classes generally do well on the math portion of the SAT I and the ACT.

Look for ways to apply math in your daily life.

Problems requiring students to interpret everyday data, calculate real-world probabilities, and otherwise apply mathematics to realistic problem situations are becoming more and more common on the SAT I and ACT. At the same time, old-style "story problems" involving age and distance are becoming rare.

The best way to learn to solve real-world problems is to begin to see math as a component of your everyday life, rather than as an irrelevant subject whose principles you must tediously memorize. Math comes alive and begins to make sense when you see it in newspapers and on billboards, when you hear it discussed at meetings and find it in the activities you do each day. Cultivate the practice of discovering math in your everyday life.

Short-term planning for both the SAT I and the ACT should include the following:

Begin a disciplined math-review program.

Use these review materials, SAT I and ACT review books you can find in the public or school library, and official publications of the SAT I and ACT boards. Set aside a specific amount of time each day for review. Make notes about questions that arise as you review, so you can ask your math teacher about them the next day.

Begin your review program four to eight weeks before you plan to take the test and continue right up to the day before the test. Then give yourself a break. Last-minute cramming the night before the test will probably not improve your test score, but it will almost certainly frazzle you. Congratulate yourself for your hard work, enjoy an evening away from your review program with your family or friends, and then get a good night's sleep.

Practice, practice, practice.

As you review, don't be satisfied with simply reading review materials and memorizing methods or procedures for solving problems. Prepare for the test by repeatedly practicing everything you'll experience on test day.

- Practice solving SAT I- or ACT-type problems again and again and again.
- If you're taking the SAT I, practice solving problems written in each question format—multiple-choice, quantitative comparison, and student-produced response. Spend extra time practicing the gridding of student-produced responses, which present so many ways to go wrong.
- Practice reading directions.
- Practice filling in answer sheets.

SAT/ACT: Test-Taking Tips

- Practice working under test conditions by setting an alarm clock and giving yourself set amounts of time to answer specific numbers of questions.

- Practice relaxing and not becoming rattled when you can't answer a question or several questions in a row.

- Practice using your calculator to solve problems.

- Practice making decisions as to whether or not you will use your calculator to solve a problem.

- Practice making decisions as to whether or not you will guess answers to questions that stump you.

- If you're taking the SAT I, practice gridding student-produced responses.

The more you practice at home what you'll actually be doing at the test site, the more the test itself will seem familiar and nonthreatening, allowing you to obtain your best possible score.

Be ready to go on the morning of the test.

Collect the following materials before test day, and put them in a place where you'll know where to find them:

- #2 pencils

- Your ID. This must include your photo or a brief description of you. A description must be written on school stationery or on a school ID form. You must sign it in front of your principal or guidance counselor, who must also sign it.

- Your admission ticket

- Your calculator, with fresh batteries

- A watch

- A healthy snack

Be sure you've scoped out ahead of time exactly how to get to the test site and how long it will take you to get there. If you rush in at the last second, you won't be relaxed and focused on taking the test. And if you rush in *after* the last second, you won't be allowed to take the test.

SAT/ACT PREPARATION

SAT/ACT: Test-Taking Tips

Taking the Test

The following are time-honored test-taking strategies.

Manage Your Time Efficiently.

The questions in each section of the test are arranged roughly in order of difficulty. As you begin, make a quick estimate of the average amount of time you have to answer each question. Use the estimate to guide you through the section. Allow yourself a little less than the average amount of time for the early, easier first questions so that you'll have extra time for the harder ones later on.

Starting with the first question, move as quickly as you can through the section. Consider each question in turn. Make a quick assessment as to whether you can solve it rapidly. If you think you can, do so. Work at a comfortable pace, but don't linger. Spending too much time on a problem in the fanciful belief that you've *almost got it* is a killer. Remember: all problems are worth the same number of points. You receive one point for each easy question that you answer correctly and one point for each hard one. How should you spend your time?

If you decide that you can probably solve a problem with a little more time, draw a circle around it. After you've made your first pass through all the questions, answering those that seem easy, return to the questions you've circled. This second look is often successful, so don't get discouraged if you find yourself circling lots of questions. Continue to pace yourself during the second pass. Work your way through the questions you think you have a chance on, but don't be reluctant to abandon them again and move on if they continue to tie you up. After the second pass, return to the questions that continue to stump you if time remains.

If you're sure that you won't be able to solve a problem, draw an **X** beside it and forget it. Throwing in the towel on questions you can't answer is simply good time management and nothing to apologize for. No one is expected to answer every question correctly and few people do.

For guidelines on guessing answers, see "Stick to a sensible guessing strategy," below.

Be careful.

Beware of the following:

- Under the pressure of test-taking, it's easy to make careless mistakes. Work through calculations methodically, rechecking them quickly at the end. Ask yourself if answers are reasonable. Is the price after a discount greater than the original price? Does one of the acute angles in a right triangle measure 150°? Use estimation whenever possible. On multiple-choice questions, an estimate may be enough to help you decide which of the given answers is correct without actually working it out.

- On multiple-choice questions, watch out for "obvious" choices. In the first part of a section, where the questions are relatively easy, an answer that seems obvious may be the right one. But in the last part, the obvious answer may have been put there to deceive you. After all, if an answer is obvious, what's the question doing in the hard part of the test?

- Check and double-check to make sure that you're writing your answers in the correct spots, and beside the correct numbers. To guard against potential disasters, many students write all their answers in their test booklets *only*, transferring them all at once to their answer sheets in the final minute or two.

- Beware of long computations. SAT I and ACT problems can usually be solved with minimal calculations. If you find yourself in the midst of a multi-step nightmare, it's best to stop and look for a shortcut—or move on to the next question.

- If you're told that a figure is not drawn to scale, believe it. Don't assume that lengths and angles are drawn accurately.

- Measurements may be given in different units. If they are, convert and work the problem in one unit.

Be smart.

Use these ideas to simplify your work and improve your score.

- Write in your test booklet. There's no reward for a clean booklet and no penalty for one that's covered with pencil marks. If a question doesn't have a drawing and one would help, draw it. Write measurements and values on the drawing. When you calculate an answer, write out your calculations so that you can check them later. The next time, try doing them a different way. This is a good way to check your work and often reveals careless mistakes.

- On multiple-choice questions, draw a line through choices you know to be wrong. This will simplify the job of choosing the right answer.

- Look at the answer choices before working a problem. This will show you the form of the answer that is required (a fraction, for example), allowing you to work the problem in that form from the beginning rather than having to rewrite your answer later in a different form.

- Under "Reference Information," the SAT I booklet provides a considerable amount of information on geometrical relationships. Use it.

- In quantitative comparisons, you may not have to evaluate each expression. You need only find which is greater. For example, which is greater: 2^{10} or 4^5? Applying rules for exponents ($4 = 2^2$, so $4^5 = 2^{10}$) you can see that the expressions are equal, even though you did not find actual values.

- Know commonly used numbers. Recognize powers of 2, 3, and 5. Know the decimal equivalents for simple fractions with denominators of 2, 3, 4, 5, 6, 8, and 10. Know the common Pythagorean triples 3-4-5 and 5-12-13 and recognize their multiples.

Use your calculator wisely.

Every test question can be answered without a calculator, so you don't have to bring one. Bring one anyway. Make it one you're familiar with and comfortable using. It can be a scientific or graphing calculator, but many students find that a simple four-function model with a square-root key works best. That's because the kinds of calculations you'll be using it for (see next page) are easier to perform on a simple calculator than they are on a Super Amazing Quasar Laser KT-4000 (you won't be asked to find log 453.779 or arcsin 0.8812 on the SAT I or ACT). Equally important, the keys on a simple calculator are easier to hit than the keys on a scientific or graphing calculator, meaning you're less likely to make a careless mistake on good old Rusty than you are on the Super Amazing.

Resist the temptation to use your calculator, or to try to use it, to solve every problem. Most of the problems on the SAT I and the ACT can be solved far more easily without a calculator than with it. Both tests are designed to test your knowledge of mathematics and your ability to solve problems, not to find out whether you know how to punch the keys on a calculator. So, in most cases, you'll save time and improve your chances of scoring points by turning to your calculator only for the specific purposes listed below, or to check your work, or when you can see no other approach.

Example

Find the product: $\frac{1}{2} \times \frac{2}{3} \times \frac{3}{4} \times \frac{4}{5} \times \frac{5}{6} \times \frac{6}{7} \times \frac{7}{8} \times \frac{8}{9}$

(A) 0.1   (B) $\frac{1}{9}$ (C) 0.11111111   (D) $\frac{1}{90}$ (E) Not given

To solve the problem, you *could* use your calculator:

$$\frac{1 \times 2 \times 3 \times 4 \times 5 \times 6 \times 7 \times 8}{2 \times 3 \times 4 \times 5 \times 6 \times 7 \times 8 \times 9} = \frac{362,880}{3,265,920} = 0.11111111 \text{ (to 8 places)}.$$

Although (C) looks right, it and your solution are rounded versions of the correct answer. To find the correct answer, you must now use your calculator again to rewrite the fraction choices $\frac{1}{9}$ and $\frac{1}{90}$ as decimals. Doing so will confirm that the correct answer is (B) $\frac{1}{9}$.

The wise test-taker will look for a more efficient solution before plunging into a messy calculation like the above. Here, the product $\frac{1}{2} \times \frac{2}{3} \times \frac{3}{4} \times \frac{4}{5} \times \frac{5}{6} \times \frac{6}{7} \times \frac{7}{8} \times \frac{8}{9}$ can be quickly simplified by noticing that every denominator except the last equals the numerator of the following fraction. Therefore, all of the figures can be divided out except the first numerator and the last denominator.

$$\frac{1}{\cancel{2}} \times \frac{\cancel{2}}{\cancel{3}} \times \frac{\cancel{3}}{\cancel{4}} \times \frac{\cancel{4}}{\cancel{5}} \times \frac{\cancel{5}}{\cancel{6}} \times \frac{\cancel{6}}{\cancel{7}} \times \frac{\cancel{7}}{\cancel{8}} \times \frac{\cancel{8}}{9} = \frac{1}{9}$$

A calculator *is* useful for doing the following, any of which you might be faced with on the test:

- finding percents;
- finding square roots;
- comparing fractions;
- rewriting fractions as decimals.

A few more calculator tips:

- If you find yourself performing complex calculations, you're probably doing something wrong. Stop and rethink your approach to the problem.

SAT/ACT: Test-Taking Tips

- When you're solving sample problems as part of your preparation for the test, practice making quick decisions as to whether or not you should use your calculator.

- Practice entering numbers on your calculator correctly. When you take the test, enter numbers deliberately and with care. Herein lies another drawback of calculators: They provide no paper trail to tell you that you pressed the wrong buttons.

- Don't forget to $\boxed{\text{CLEAR}}$ after you finish performing a calculation.

Stick to a sensible guessing strategy.

Guessing on the ACT

Your score on the ACT is based on the number of questions you answer correctly. No points are deducted for incorrect answers. Therefore, you should answer every question, even those that stump you. As you take the test, mark the questions you can't answer. Return to them after you've answered as many questions as you can and give those that puzzle you a second try. In the final seconds before you are told to stop, fill in the blank spaces on your answer sheet with random guesses.

To see why this strategy makes sense, consider Bill and Phil, both of whom are completely boggled by 20 questions on the math portion of the ACT.

- Bill left all 20 questions unanswered.

Score:	0 correct	=	0 points
	0 incorrect	=	0 points
	Total	=	0 points

- Phil guessed the answers to all 20. The probability of guessing the correct answer from among 5 choices is one-fifth, and, indeed, Phil guessed $20 \cdot \frac{1}{5} = 4$ correctly.

Score:	4 correct	=	4 points
	16 incorrect	=	0 points
	Total	=	4 points

Phil outscored Bill by 4 points. On the ACT, guessing answers to questions that totally stump you is likely to improve your score.

Guessing on the SAT I

There is widespread confusion about whether or not to guess answers to multiple-choice questions on the SAT I. Much of the confusion is caused by the mistaken understanding that guessers are somehow penalized beyond the bounds of probability by a mysterious "guessing penalty."

In fact, there is no extra penalty for guessing on the SAT I. Again, consider Bill and Phil, now taking the SAT I. Once more, they're unable to answer 20 questions, each with 5 answer choices.

- Bill left all 20 questions unanswered.

Score:	0 correct	=	0 points
	0 incorrect	=	0 points
	Total	=	0 points

- Phil guessed the answers to all 20 questions. As before, he guessed correctly on exactly the number of questions that chance predicts, $20 \cdot \frac{1}{5} = 4$.

Score:	4 correct	=	4 points	
	16 incorrect	=	$(-)4$ points	$(16 \times \frac{1}{4} = 4)$
	Total	=	0 points	

Bill and Phil both earned 0 points for their efforts. The conclusion is this: If you are *completely* stumped by an SAT I multiple-choice question—that is, if all 5 (or 4) answers appear equally likely to be correct—it makes no difference in the long run whether you guess the answer or leave the space blank on your answer sheet.

The arguments against guessing in such situations are mostly subjective. The *knowledge* that you're guessing answers blindly may begin to weigh on your mind, affecting your ability to do your best on the test. And, of course, you waste a tiny amount of time filling in your answer sheet with random guesses. You're likely to do just as well leaving the spaces blank.

Improving the Odds

As you've seen, the odds are that guessing blindly on multiple-choice questions that are complete stumpers won't hurt you on either the ACT or the SAT I; on the ACT, it will probably help you.

But you're not going to impress any college admissions officers with a score obtained through blind guessing. That brings us to a sensible guessing strategy over which you have some control, and one that is likely to improve your score: **Eliminate first and then guess**.

If you can eliminate just one of the given answers to a question as definitely wrong, it's to your advantage to guess from among the remaining choices. If you can eliminate two answers, it's *strongly* to your advantage to guess. If you can eliminate three answers, *you're very foolish not to guess*. (If you can eliminate four answers, the one you didn't eliminate is the answer!)

The reason that this kind of educated guessing makes sense is that, following elimination, the potential gain from a correct answer chosen through blind luck exceeds the potential deduction for an incorrect answer. The more answers you can eliminate, the greater the gap between potential gain and potential loss.

Therefore, on multiple-choice questions for which you cannot choose the correct answer, you should follow this strategy: Eliminate as many answers as possible, and then guess. This strategy makes sense on both the SAT I and the ACT. (And on the ACT, don't forget to randomly fill in *all* blank spaces before you're told to put down your pencil. On the SAT I there's no need to do that, though the odds are that you'll suffer no penalty if you do.)

SAT/ACT: Practice Test

Section I Multiple Choice

In the following problems you have five choices for an answer. Only one choice is correct. On the SAT I or ACT, you will mark your choice on the special answer sheet. Your teacher will provide you with a sample answer sheet.

1 If $x - 4 = x^2 - 6$, then $x =$

(A) 1 or 2

(B) -1 or 2

(C) 0 or 2

(D) -1 or -2

(E) -1 or 4

2 If a square is copied beside itself to produce a rectangle, $\dfrac{\text{perimeter of rectangle}}{\text{perimeter of square}} =$

(A) 4

(B) 3

(C) 2

(D) 1.5

(E) 1

3 Mark bought 14 tapes, some priced at $6 each and the rest priced at $8 each. If he spent $94 altogether, how many tapes did he buy at each price?

(A) 6 at $6 and 8 at $8

(B) 7 at $6 and 7 at $8

(C) 8 at $6 and 6 at $8

(D) 9 at $6 and 5 at $8

(E) 10 at $6 and 4 at $8

4 If $\dfrac{x - 2}{x + 2} = \dfrac{1}{2}$, then $x =$

(A) 2

(B) 3

(C) 4

(D) 5

(E) 6

5 Jorge bought 16 CDs at a cost of $9 each. How many $12 CDs could he have bought for the amount he paid?

(A) 8

(B) 9

(C) 10

(D) 12

(E) 21

6 Five people split the following costs equally among themselves:

$12.40, $10.95, $16.75, $6.10.

How much did each person pay?

(A) $9.24

(B) $11.55

(C) $20.22

(D) $33.21

(E) $66.42

7 Jason worked 20 hours at $5 per hour and 30 hours at $6 per hour. What was his average hourly wage?

(A) $5.20

(B) $5.40

(C) $5.50

(D) $5.60

(E) $5.65

8 $2^2 + (2^3)^2 = \underline{\ ?\ }$

(A) $(2^2)17$

(B) 2^7

(C) 2^8

(D) 10^2

(E) $2^2(5)$

SAT/ACT PREPARATION

GO ON

9 $x^2 - 4 = 3x$. Then $x = $ ___?___

(A) 2 or -2

(B) 0

(C) 4 or -1

(D) 3 or 0

(E) 2, -2, or 0

10 In simplified form, $\dfrac{x^6 + x^4}{x^2}$ equals

(A) $x^3 + x^2$

(B) $x^4 + x^2$

(C) x^5

(D) x^8

(E) x^{12}

11 Ted bought 3 books at m dollars each. The sales tax on his purchase was 5% of the cost of the books. Which of the following expresses the total cost of his purchase?

(A) $15m$

(B) $0.15m$

(C) $18m$

(D) $3.15m$

(E) $3m + 0.05$

12 If $-5x \geq 20$, which of the following is true?

(A) $x \leq 15$

(B) $x \leq 4$

(C) $x \leq -4$

(D) $x \geq 15$

(E) $x \geq -4$

GO ON

13 Which of the following pairs (x, y) is a solution of the system?

$$x + y = 4$$
$$-x + 2y = -1$$

(A) $(1, 3)$

(B) $(3, 1)$

(C) $(2, 2)$

(D) $(5, -1)$

(E) $(-2, 6)$

15 A line segment is drawn from $A(14, 10)$ to $B(6, 4)$. Find the distance from A to the midpoint of the segment.

(A) 3

(B) 4

(C) 5

(D) 6

(E) 8

14 If $\dfrac{1}{a + b} = 5$, then $b = $ ____?____

(A) $\dfrac{1}{5} - a$

(B) $-5a$

(C) $1 - a$

(D) $\dfrac{1 + 5a}{5}$

(E) $\dfrac{1 - a}{5}$

16 Where does the line $6x - 2y = -10$ cross the y-axis?

(A) -10

(B) $-\dfrac{5}{3}$

(C) 3

(D) 5

(E) 10

GO ON

SAT/ACT: Practice Test

Section I Multiple Choice (Continued)

17 Which of the following points are on the line $y = 3x - 5$?

I. $(2, -1)$
II. $(4, 3)$
III. $(0, -5)$

(A) I only

(B) II only

(C) III only

(D) I and III only

(E) II and III only

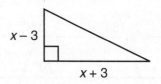

19 For what value of x is the area of the above triangle equal to 36?

(A) $3\sqrt{2}$

(B) 3

(C) $3\sqrt{5}$

(D) 9

(E) 12

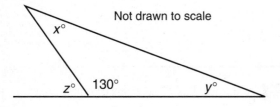

Not drawn to scale

18 Which statements could be true for this figure?

I. $z = x + y$
II. $z > y$
III. $z = x$

(A) I only

(B) II only

(C) I and II only

(D) II and III only

(E) I, II, and III

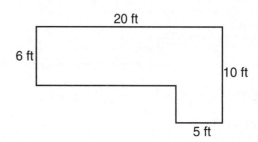

20 The perimeter of the above figure, in feet, is

(A) 200

(B) 140

(C) 60

(D) 52

(E) 41

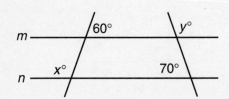

21 In the figure above, $m \parallel n$. What is the sum $x + y$?

(A) 130

(B) 180

(C) 200

(D) 230

(E) 270

23 The areas of the four sectors of the spinner are equal. The probability of spinning C *and* tossing a head with a penny is

(A) 8

(B) 1

(C) $\frac{3}{4}$

(D) $\frac{1}{2}$

(E) $\frac{1}{8}$

22 The expression $\dfrac{\sin^2 x + \cos^2 x}{\sec x}$ simplifies to

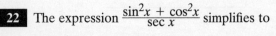

(A) $\sin x$

(B) $\cos x$

(C) $\tan x$

(D) $\sec x$

(E) $\csc x$

24 A spinner has 12 sections of equal area. The probability of spinning red is $\frac{1}{3}$ and the probability of spinning red or yellow is $\frac{3}{4}$. The number of yellow sections is

(A) 2

(B) 4

(C) 5

(D) 6

(E) 9

STOP

SAT/ACT: Practice Test

Section II *Quantitative Comparison*

Each problem in this section consists of a quantity in Column A and a quantity in Column B. Sometimes, as in Problem 1, there is information preceding the two columns.

Compare the two quantities and mark your sample answer sheet as follows:

(A) means the quantity in Column A is greater.
(B) means the quantity in Column B is greater.
(C) means the two quantities are equal.
(D) means the relationship cannot be determined from the information given.
(E) is never to be marked in this part, even though there is an "E" bubble on the answer sheet.

1 x is a real number

Column A	Column B
$3x$	$2x + 4$

3   perimeter of square $PQRS = 8x$

Column A	Column B
side of $PQRS$	$3x$

2

Column A	Column B
$\dfrac{5}{14} + \dfrac{31}{14}$	$\dfrac{18}{7}$

4   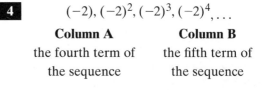 $(-2), (-2)^2, (-2)^3, (-2)^4, \ldots$

Column A	Column B
the fourth term of the sequence	the fifth term of the sequence

5

Column A	Column B
the distance between $(5, 1)$ and $(8, -4)$	the distance between $(6, 2)$ and $(3, 7)$

6

$$x + 4 = 3x - 3$$

Column A	Column B
$2x$	$x + 1$

7

Column A	Column B
$\sin 60°$	$\cos 60°$

8

Column A	Column B
the number of pairs of corresponding angles formed by two parallel lines and a transversal	the number of pairs of same-side interior angles formed by three parallel lines and a transversal

STOP

SAT/ACT: Practice Test

Section III Student-Produced Responses

After you solve each problem on this section, enter your answer on the special grid of your sample answer sheet.

1 What is the greatest value out of $\frac{3}{10}$, 0.03, and $\frac{2}{5}$?

3 The product of $(5 - 1)$, $(5 - 2)$, and $(5 - 3)$ equals twice the sum of x and 5. Then $x = $ ___?___

2 If $\frac{1}{x} = \sqrt{0.04}$, then x equals ___?___

4 Find the value of $n^4 - n^3$ when $n = -3$.

5 What is the positive solution to
$2x^2 - 5x - 3 = 0$?

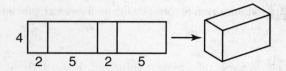

7 The figure on the left is folded to form a bottomless, topless box. If a top and bottom are put on the box, what is their combined area?

6 What is the sum of the measures of the interior angles of a 6-sided polygon?

8 The areas of two similar triangles are 98 in.^{2} and 162 in.^{2}. What is the ratio of their perimeters when comparing smaller to larger?

SAT/ACT PREPARATION

9 Two-thirds of 24 is equal to 25 percent of what number?

10 What is the constant term

of $\dfrac{3x^4 + 9x^3 - 2x^2 + 18}{x + 3}$?

STOP